1

I Feel Worried:

Tips for Kids on Overcoming Anxiety

Authors Nadine Briggs and Donna Shea

Copyright © 2016 How to Make and Keep Friends, LLC

ISBN-13: 978-0997280814
ISBN-10: 0997280816

We make every effort to identify original sources for tips that we share. Many ideas can be found in some form in the public domain. If you are aware of an original source for an idea, please let us know and we will make sure to cite it.

What is worry? It is when your brain becomes stuck on something and decides that it needs to be afraid. Brains do not always make sense, and sometimes feeling worried can be a waste of your time and your energy and can prevent you from being your happiest self.

Worry is also known as:

Stress, Fear, or Anxiety.

Sometimes your brain can become stuck on a thought that plays over and over in a loop. A thought that is stuck might be a worry and you might not even be aware of it!

The thing about worried thoughts is that you never want them to make decisions for you. If you have a brain that gets stuck on thoughts, especially if it gets stuck on bad thoughts that cause you to avoid some good things, then this book is for you. We will help you conquer your worries. This book will teach you how to fight back as an expert worry ninja.

Becoming a worry ninja means that you can learn to manage those worried feelings and get them out of your way. You can be stronger and more powerful than the worry.

Your brain is taking in information all of the time. It has to decide which things are dangerous or bad and which things are okay. A brain can become confused and get it wrong. This book will help teach your brain to get it right!

WHAT YOU WILL NEED
to become a powerful worry ninja!

 Your brain ready to take control!

 A pencil to write down ideas.

 A healthy snack is always nice!

FIRST, IF YOU HAVE A BRAIN THAT WORRIES A LOT, WE WANT YOU TO KNOW THAT:

1) no worry is too weird, and we guarantee that someone else has had the same stuck thought as you, and

2) you should never worry alone.

Do you wonder if worry is ever a useful feeling? The correct answer is yes! Worry is very useful if you are in an unsafe situation. It can make sure that you take action to stay safe.

For example, if you are crossing a street and a car comes zooming past you, feeling worried about the car getting too close can help you to get out of the way. You definitely need that type of worry to stay safe.

If your brain begins worrying when you are not in danger, then that is when worrying can become a problem. Your body might feel worry in ways that you do not expect. You might feel physically REALLY uncomfortable. You could experience:

Your face blushing
Blurry vision
A lump in your throat
Losing your words
Feeling smothered
Ringing in your ears
Pain in your chest

Diarrhea
Shortness of breath
Tightness in your chest
Irritability
Meanness
A headache
A stomachache
Dizziness
Feeling as though the room is too small
Feeling as though it is too noisy
Feeling like you want to hide
Feeling like you want to yell or scream
A floating feeling
Tearfulness
Tingly sensations
Feeling cold or hot
Weakness
Nausea or vomiting
Shakiness
Yawning or sleepiness
Butterflies in your stomach
Sweaty palms
Your heart beating fast

DRAW OR COLOR HOW YOUR BODY FEELS WHEN *YOU* ARE GETTING WORRIED.

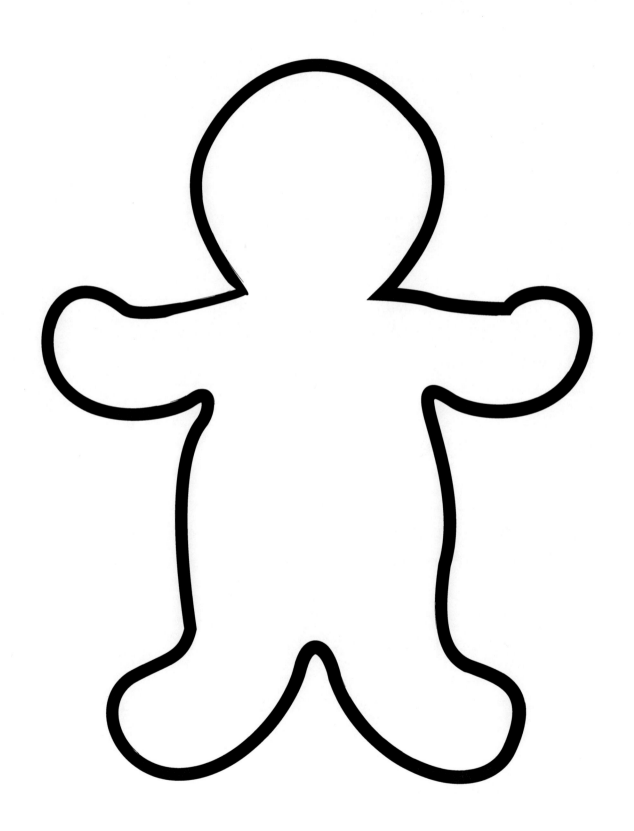

UNDERSTANDING EMOTIONS

It is important to understand the emotions you are feeling and know that it is okay to feel them. The trick to keeping emotions from becoming too strong is to catch them and manage them before they become gigantic. Here are a few ways to help you figure out what you are feeling:

EMOTIONS CHARADES

Emotions charades can be great fun to play as a class or for family game night. One person acts out an emotion using only facial expressions and body language (no talking) and the rest of the group has to guess what the first player is feeling. You can find a list of emotions that you can use to play this game in the appendix.

FEELINGS COLLAGE

Look through old magazines or online with a parent for pictures of emotions. Cut them out and glue them onto a piece of poster board. Label each emotion and talk about a time when you or someone close to you felt that way.

WATCH TV WITH THE SOUND OFF

Another fun way to practice understanding emotions is to watch TV with the sound turned off. Watch the actors to see if you can figure out what is going on in the show, what the characters are feeling and why, just by watching their faces and body language.

EMOTION WHEEL

Draw a wheel with common emotions listed on it. Take a small pebble or object and toss it onto the wheel. Read out the name of the emotion that it landed on and discuss a time when you felt that emotion. Play with your parents or another adult and learn how they handled these emotions when they felt them. Use the emotions listed in the appendix to create your own emotion wheel.

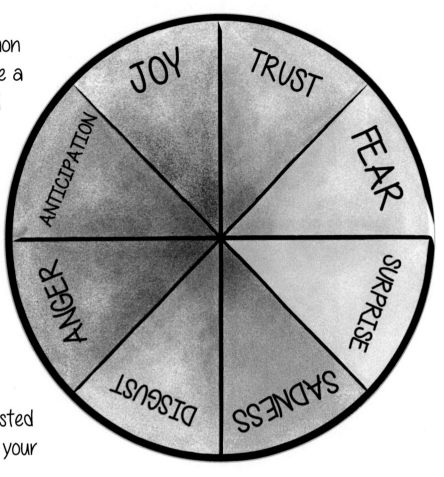

PRACTICE FACIAL EXPRESSIONS IN MIRROR

Practice acting out feelings in the mirror and see what they look like on your own face. Can you name what these characters are feeling?

9

WHAT MAKES YOU WORRY?

Bullying

Teasing

Not understanding what is happening
or expected

Loud noises

Strong smells

Foods that you do not want to eat

Not having friends

Not understanding what someone
wants from you

School work that is hard

Not knowing how to spend
your free time

Feeling different from other kids

Understanding social media (text
messages or things that people post)

Changes to your schedule or routine

New experiences

Not being able to do your favorite
thing

When other people touch you

When you feel like running around
but you are not supposed to run
around

Losing at a game

Waiting for your turn

Someone using or taking your stuff

Playdates or sleepovers

The dark

Shadows

Wondering what is in the closet

Wondering what is under your bed

Fighting or arguments

You might not even know what causes your worry. It might just be a stuck
thought that you cannot seem to stop thinking about.

FILL IN WHAT MAKES YOU WORRY:

_____

_____

_____

I Feel Worried! Tips for Kids on Overcoming Anxiety

IS WORRY REAL?

The emotion that you feel when you worry **is** real, but most worry is about something that only **might** happen. Most worried thoughts start with the words:

WHAT IF...

"What if I say something embarrassing?"

"What if it's really loud?"

"What if I get into trouble?"

"What if people don't like me?"

"What if others get mad at me?"

"What if I get hurt?"

"What if I'm not as good as everyone else?"

"What if I feel something bad will happen?"

"What if I get laughed at?"

"What if I don't know what to do?"

"What if I break the rules?"

"What if I'm afraid to ask a question?"

"What if I don't know anyone there?"

Many of the things kids worry about are addressed in our book,
How to Make and Keep Friends: Tips for Kids to Overcome 50 Common Social Challenges.

WHAT ARE *YOUR* "WHAT IF" THOUGHTS?

_____

_____

_____

_____

ARE THESE THOUGHTS USEFUL? _____

Some "what if" thoughts help you to feel prepared. For example, you might wonder "what if" you forget your lines in a play. If you have this "what if" thought, you can think about what you can do if you do forget your lines. That would be helpful!

Write about a time when a "what if" thought was helpful to you.

_____

_____

_____

_____

"Worrying is like a rocking chair, it gives you something to do, but it gets you nowhere. "

~Glenn Turner

The important thing is, you really should not let the worries win. You may not feel as though you are stronger than your worries, but you really and truly are!

How can you fight back? Your brain is your best power tool! Freeze your brain and stomp out those worried thoughts by thinking:

"I can and will control the thoughts in my brain."

Most worries can be overcome by replacing the worried thought with a coping thought. A coping thought is a plan or a strategy to handle your worry or problem. Let's practice coping thoughts for a few common worries together.

THE WORRY: I may need a shot when I go to the doctor next time and it will hurt.

COPING THOUGHTS:

- I will imagine myself as a brave worry ninja feeling great while getting the shot.

- I will pretend that I have cooked noodles for arms and keep them loose and floppy so it doesn't hurt as much.

- I will remind myself that the pain is not that bad and is super quick.

- I can ask the doctor or nurse questions to gather the facts.

- I will remember that a shot is way better than getting sick.

-  _____

_____

HERE'S ANOTHER ONE!

THE WORRY: Because of an assembly, the schedule is different at school today. Changes in my schedule worry me. I worry that there are more changes that I don't know about or that I won't know what to do when they happen.

COPING THOUGHTS:

- I can write down the new schedule so I don't forget.

- I can remember that assemblies are fun.

- I will see friends from other classes.

- I will take three deep belly breaths to relax my body.

- I will remind myself that it's just for today.

- I can fill out a change in routine card from this book.

-

-

AND ANOTHER!

THE WORRY: I have a playdate at a new friend's house and I've never been there before.

COPING THOUGHTS:

- I will deal with whatever comes my way. I am strong and powerful!

- I can decide to be friendly and focus on having a new friend instead of my worry.

- If I have any questions, I can ask my friend for help.

- My friend might feel nervous, too.

- I can think about how I would help my friend with a worry and do the same thing.

- _____
  _____

- _____
  _____

I Feel Worried! Tips for Kids on Overcoming Anxiety

TRY ONE MORE!

THE WORRY: I hope my science project is good enough. I tried to make it perfect but what if it isn't?

COPING THOUGHTS:

- I can only try to do my best. No one is perfect.

- I will imagine that I can handle things as well as someone I respect.

- I can decide to stop the worrying and take action to solve my problems.

- Even if my project isn't the best it could be, it probably won't be the worst.

- If I'm not happy with my grade, I can always ask for help the next time. It's always OK to ask for help.

- Some other kids probably feel the same way I do.

- _____

- _____

A WORRY NINJA TOOL KIT

You can help fight back worry thoughts by creating a Worry Ninja Tool Kit! Here are some ideas for what to put in your kit. (Some ideas are for inside your brain and some are for outside your brain.) Choose the ones that are right for you or do them all. It's up to you.

SCAVENGER HUNT TOOLS

Search your brain for facts to prove that the worry you have is likely to happen. Write down those facts in a notebook. Next, search for facts to prove that the worry is unlikely to happen and write those down in the notebook, too. Which list is longer?

WORRY: DAD IS LATE PICKING ME UP AND I'M WORRIED HE'S NOT COMING	
FACTS: LIKELY TO HAPPEN	**FACTS: UNLIKELY TO HAPPEN**
ANYTHING IS POSSIBLE	HE'S NEVER FORGOTTEN BEFORE
	HE'S BEEN LATE IF TRAFFIC IS BAD, BUT HAS SHOWN UP
	HE TOLD ME THIS MORNING THAT HE WOULD PICK ME UP SO I KNOW HE REMEMBERED

VOICE ACTIVATED BRAIN

Inside your head, activate your brain to tell yourself to switch channels to some other thoughts or to clear your head of any thoughts altogether.

To clear your thoughts, try listening to the sounds around you including the sound of your breathing. Try to focus only on those sounds.

PRACTICE RELAXING YOUR BODY ONE PART AT A TIME
TRY THIS WHEN YOU ARE TRYING TO FALL ASLEEP:

- Find a steady and slow deep breathing rhythm, in and out.

- Think of your toes feeling really heavy and tired

- Now pretend your legs are super sleepy and can't move off of the bed or floor.

- Press your back into the bed or floor as though it is stuck there forever.

- Think about your arms feeling like big weights that you can't lift.

- Pretend your head is now a big heavy coconut laying in the sand

- ZZZZZZ

WORRY BOX

Take an inexpensive container and decorate the outside with permanent marker. Write your worries down on paper and place them in the box. Seal it tight with the lid. Ask your mom or dad or guardian to set aside some time to talk about the worries that are in the box. Remember, you do not want to worry alone! When you are done talking about the worries, put them back in the box and tell yourself that you will only think of them when it's time and until then, put them in your worry locker, the next tool in your toolkit.

A WORRY NINJA TOOL KIT

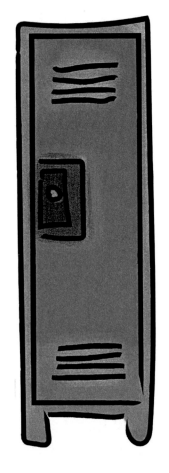

WORRY LOCKER IN YOUR BRAIN

Pretend that you have a locker in your brain. This locker is bulletproof, fireproof, waterproof, and whatever-you-want-to-call-it proof. Put your worries in your locker and then shut and lock the door. Even if you have a lot of worries, they will all fit. The locker is as big as you need it to be. Only open the locker when you have a parent, guardian, or adult with you to discuss the worries.

For both the worry box and the worry locker in your brain, if you feel the need to take the worries out, try to take them out only in the morning, after school, or around dinner time. Never take the worries out while getting ready to go to sleep or the worried thoughts might keep you awake. Remember that you are not alone. Check the worries in your box and locker over time. You might find that you are not worried about those things anymore.

If you find worries that you no longer worry about, that's awesome! This means that you overcame your worries! Congratulations! Celebrate!

BREATHE

You're probably thinking "um... I am breathing or I would be passed out on the floor so... next tool, please!" We know that you are breathing, but calm breathing is very different from regular old breathing. It is the quickest, easiest, and most important thing you can do to begin to calm down. Breathing to calm down your worry needs to be really slow.

Breathe in slowly while counting to 5 in your head

Hold your breath in while counting to 5 in your head

Breathe out slowly while counting to 5 in your head

Once you have done this slow breathing one, two, or even three times, count to ten in your head just to make sure you have calmed yourself down. It may help to picture a calm scene in your head.

WHAT IS YOUR CALM SCENE? DRAW IT HERE:

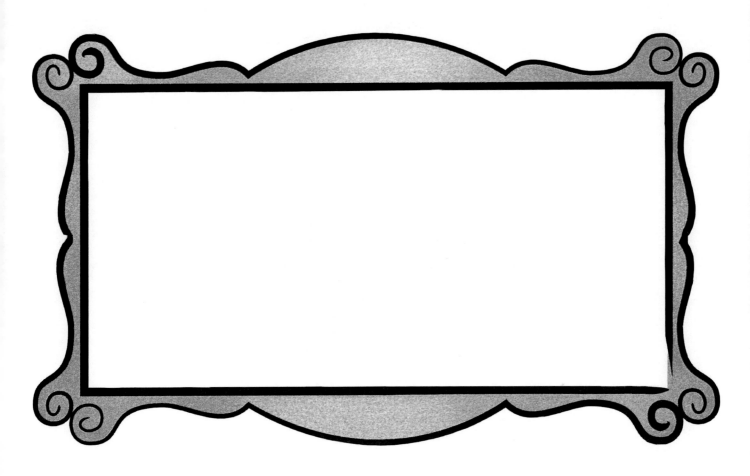

COMFORT ZONE POSTER

To help you sleep at night, create
a Comfort Zone poster. Draw
two sleepy eyes at the top of your
poster board to start. Then draw
or cut out pictures from magazines
of things that make you feel happy.
Hang this by your bed and look at
it while falling asleep.

WORRY TUBES

Decorate the outside of an empty cardboard tube. Write your worry on a
small piece of paper and crunch it into a ball. Toss the crumpled up worry into
the worry tube "chamber" for a little attitude adjustment.

CHANGE IN ROUTINE CARDS

Worries can happen if there is a change to your schedule. You might spend a lot of time thinking about the change to make sure you don't forget it. That could make you worry about it. Try these Change in Routine Cards the next time you have a schedule change. Once the change is written down, you won't need to keep it inside your head. This will allow your brain to think about other things.

CHANGE IN ROUTINE CARDS

The change or new routine is:

_____

If this makes you feel worried:
1. Tell yourself it is going to be OK.
2. Breathe slowly and deeply.
3. Tell yourself you are stronger and more powerful than the worry.
4. Try _____ (Fill in your own idea)

For example:

CHANGE IN ROUTINE CARDS

The change or new routine is:

I am getting picked up instead of taking the bus.

If this makes you feel worried:
1. Tell yourself it is going to be OK.
2. Breathe slowly and deeply.
3. Tell yourself you are stronger and more powerful than the worry.
4. Try _____ (Fill in your own idea)

CALMING KIT

Create calming kits for use at home, in the car, or anywhere else you might worry. The calming kit should include things that make you feel, well... calm! Below are some ideas but be creative and put things that work for you into your kit.

Chewing gum

Modeling clay

Notebook or pad to write down feelings

Worry tube

A soft, cuddly stuffed animal

Earmuffs or earplugs to block out annoying or loud sounds

Something to fidget with such as a rubber tube or worry ball

Weighted blanket

A favorite book

Music

Video game

Snack

Encouragement cards (find them in the appendix)

Worry dice (also in the appendix)

Social story

Lavender-scented pillow

Worry stone

Put your ideas for your own calming kit here:

_____

_____

GRATITUDE BOX

When you focus on the things that make you happy, or the things for which you are grateful, you train your brain to focus on the positive. Take a plastic container or some other kind of box and decorate the outside with permanent marker. On small pieces of paper, write down things that make you feel happy. Fold up the notes and put them in the box. You could add things to the box that you are grateful for in the morning and then add all the things that went great during the day before you go to bed at night. Need some ideas? Here are things some kids enjoy:

Snuggling your pet

Snuggling your stuffed animals

Snuggling your mom, dad, or guardian

Warm sunshine on your face

Swimming in a pool

Laughing with friends

Your favorite flavor of ice cream

Making s'mores by a fire pit

Singing a song

Dancing

Dressing up

Playing with toys

What are some things that make you happy?

_____

_____

THE AWESOME SQUAD™

We call all of the characters in our books our Awesome Squad™. In addition to our Awesome Squad™, you have your very own Awesome Squad™ to help you, too!

When you feel scared, think of the people in your life who seem to handle feeling scared or worried really well. Think to yourself,
"What would _____ do?"

Your personal Awesome Squad™ can be anybody you love or trust. There are also people whose job it is to help with worries like therapists and counselors.

MOM

PASTOR RUSSELL

GRANDPA

MR. SMITH

DAD

NANA

UNCLE FRED

Who is in your personal Awesome Squad™?

_____

_____

_____

ENCOURAGEMENT CARDS (find them in the appendix)

Copy the cards in the appendix on card stock or create your own using index cards. Laminate them if you want them to be really sturdy! Use a hole punch to make a hole in each card, then put them on a ring, or tie them together with a string. Read the cards when you feel scared or worried to remind yourself that you are stronger and more powerful than your worry is.

COPING SCENARIO

Writing down a scenario or a story about your worry can help you to understand what is making you feel worried. Maybe you need to have some surgery. That can be a scary thing to go through, but it doesn't have to take over all of your thoughts. You can write a story that starts with pictures of you before the surgery. Then put in pictures of your surgeon, you sleeping during the surgery, and another one showing you on your way to the recovery room when it is all over. Then add a happy ending picture of you being just as you were before the surgery. Even happy things like going on a long vacation can create worries. A storyline of pictures can really help when you have something big going on. Each time you write down what is bothering you and think of ways to cope, you take control over your worries!

MARBLE JAR

Overcoming worries and being a worry ninja can be hard work. Keep yourself motivated and on track with your ninja training by using a marble jar. You will need two jars. Label one with your name and the other with your worry. Every time you make a positive step toward overcoming your worry, move a marble from the worry jar to the one with your name on it. The marbles you add to the jar with your name on it will show you your success in taking back the power that your worry tries to steal!

TRUE LIST

On a piece of paper, write down all your good qualities. Are you nice? Helpful? Honest? Write down all the good things about you. The list can be as long as you want it to be and you can keep adding to it. Need some ideas? See the appendix for True List ideas.

If someone doesn't sit with you at lunch today, which of the qualities on your True List should be erased? None! You are all of these great things no matter how bad your day is or how other people treat you. Keep your list in your pocket or backpack for whenever you need to read it as a reminder of how terrific you are!

Honest
Funny
Kind
Silly
Caring

BACK OF THE DOOR REMINDER

If you have a fear or a worry that you think about almost every day, take two pieces of paper and label them like the pictures below. Tape the paper on the back of the door of your bedroom. Every time your worry doesn't happen, put a checkmark on the "DIDN'T happen" sheet of paper. Every time your worry does happen, put a check mark on the "happened" sheet of paper. If it does actually happen, also write down how bad it was on a scale of 1-10. You might see a pattern. Things you worry about might occasionally happen, but they often aren't nearly as bad as you thought they would be.

Worries That Happened Today

Worries That Didn't Happen Today

GRUDGES

Do you know what causes a lot of worry and takes up a lot of time and energy? Holding a grudge. A grudge is when you stay upset about something whether the other person has apologized or not. You might continue to have thoughts about it long after it is all over. Grudges are not healthy to keep or hold on to. Remember that everyone does things they shouldn't do sometimes, and chances are that even you needed forgiveness at some point. Here is a simple way to get rid of a grudge:

Write your grudge or grudges (if you have a bunch) on an index card, then rip the card to shreds and throw it away in the trash or recycling bin. Once it hits the trash, tell yourself you are all done thinking about that bad thing. The grudge should be gone forever! If it's not, you might want to talk it out with a trusted adult.

EXERCISE

Exercise is a great way to manage stress and anxiety. Go outside and run, ride your bike, shoot hoops, or swing on a swing set. Exercise can brighten your mood and help to manage worries.

DO THE MATH

Some kids have had one or two bad things happen to them and then continue to worry about those bad things happening again for months, or even years. A little bit of math can help. Let's use bee stings as an example. If you were stung by a bee once, should you be terrified of bees for the rest of your life? Let's say you are 10 years old and you got stung one time during your entire life.

At 10 years old, you have been
alive for about 3,650 days.
Bee Sting Days Score = 1
No Bee Sting Days Score = 3649

The No Bee Sting Days Score wins by a landslide! You can choose to focus on all of those No Bee Sting Days and not the one day you were stung.

REWARD SYSTEM

Ask your parents about getting small rewards for overcoming your fears and anxiety. You can work out your own system or try the one in the appendix.

ONE POINT
AWARD
COUPON
Choose an item off the list or save coupons for a bonus item!

THREE POINTS
BONUS
AWARD COUPON
Earn bonus coupons and choose an item off the list

31

LIVE IN THE MOMENT (ALSO CALLED "BEING MINDFUL" OR "MINDFULNESS")

Try to keep your thoughts on what is going on right now, not what has happened in the past or what is going to happen in the future. When you breathe in and out, listen to the breath coming in your mouth or nose. Concentrate on how the air feels as it fills your lungs, and then listen to it as it leaves your lungs and you breathe back out. Do the same thing when you eat. Touch and smell the food before you eat it. Feel the tasty food in your mouth and on your tongue before you swallow it. Clear everything else from your mind and focus only on what is happening right in that moment.

WALK AND TALK STRONG

Even if you are not feeling strong, put your shoulders back, stand up tall, and walk with confidence. Speak confidently, without shouting, to show the world and yourself that you really are strong. The more you practice doing this, the more it will become a part of who you really are!

PROBABLE OR POSSIBLE

Many things are definitely possible, but are they probably going to happen? Every time you go outside, it is possible that a bee could sting you, but that doesn't happen to everyone each time you step outside. It **probably** isn't going to happen.

I Feel Worried! Tips for Kids on Overcoming Anxiety

WATCH OUT FOR THE "YEAH BUTS!"

Be careful that you don't get a sneaky case of the Yeah Buts! What are the Yeah Buts? When you are given tons of strategies to help you manage your worry and you respond with "yeah... but..." followed by why you think it won't work. There are lots of strategies in this book and we're sure more than a few can help you if you give them a solid try.

Being able to manage your worries is an important skill to learn. It can make you feel healthier, happier and better able to deal with whatever comes your way. Not addressing worried thoughts can feel like running down a really steep hill only to realize that you are running way too fast.

Many kids who have lots of worried thoughts struggle with it because they want to feel in control. If you want to feel more in control, then use the tips in this book to become a worry ninja. Banish the thoughts from your brain that make you feel out of control.

Remember, you are in charge of your own life. Choosing to find happiness by managing your worries can be really hard work but it will change your life in very positive and powerful ways. Everyone is different and will find different tips useful to combat their worries. Pick a few tips to practice, and master, and you will be well on your way to becoming a worry ninja!

You hold the power in your brain to make your life better by winning over those worries!

APPENDIX
ENCOURAGEMENT CARDS

JUST BE WHO YOU ARE!

STOP, RELAX, BREATHE SLOWLY, DEEPLY, SOFTLY

YOU'RE SAFE. YOU'RE FINE.

TRY YOUR BEST IN ALL YOU DO!

YOU ARE STRONG AND POWERFUL!

YOU'RE DOING GREAT. IT'S OK!

YOUR FAMILY LOVES YOU, NO MATTER WHAT!

BELIEVE IN YOURSELF! YOU ARE A SUPER STAR!

FEELINGS CUBE

Fold and glue this die. Roll it and discuss what you would do to cope with the feeling. Adults can share ideas on how they have handled that feeling.

TRUE LIST IDEAS

Use this list for ideas to write your True List, or copy it and circle the ones that apply to you.

Friendly	Polite
Appreciative	Happy
Quiet	Outgoing
Sometimes Shy	Confident
Responsible	Goal-Oriented
Persistent	Beautiful
Brave	Strong
Powerful	Hard Worker
Enthusiastic	Sweet
Loving	Empathic
Smart	Respectful
Proud	Helpful
Bright	Compassionate
Funny	Supportive
Talented	Independent

I Feel Worried! Tips for Kids on Overcoming Anxiety

EMOTIONS CHARADES

EMOTIONS CHARADES

EMOTIONS CHARADES

REWARD COUPONS FOR WHEN YOU WIN OVER WORRIES!

ONE RULE: NO ASKING FOR COUPONS - EVER!

Prize	Coupons Needed
Having a sleepover	20
Taking a bubble bath with toys	10
Five minutes of extra screen time	5
Dinner in front of the TV	10
Going out to dinner with the family	30
Have a game night with the family	10
Inviting friends over for pizza	8
Taking a trip to the dollar store	5
Choice from the secret Prize Vault	10

ONE POINT
AWARD
COUPON

Choose an item off the list or save coupons for a bonus item!

THREE POINTS
BONUS
AWARD COUPON

Earn bonus coupons and choose an item off the list

COPY ONTO CARD STOCK AND CREATE YOUR OWN BOARD GAME!

WORRIED THOUGHT	COPING THOUGHTS
My clothes can make me feel squirmy. What should I do?	I am in control of my own life and, if I don't like something, I can take steps to change it. I can ask mom to help me find comfortable clothes.
I'm going to a new school and I'm worried I will get lost and not be able to find my classes.	I will imagine that I can handle things as well as someone I respect on my Awesome Squad™.
What if I feel embarrassed?	I'll ask for help if I need it. It's always OK to ask for help.
What if I'm in class and I don't know anybody?	I will try to say hello to just one person. If that doesn't work, I will try another person.
What if kids bully me or act in a mean way?	I'll just say "what ev" if someone is bothering me or someone is not being nice.
My friend wants me to go to the zoo this weekend but I'm worried the animals will escape from their cages!	I will imagine myself being brave and being great at something that usually scares me. I know the probability of the animals escaping is really close to zero.

WORRIED THOUGHTS

COPING THOUGHTS

WORRIED THOUGHTS	COPING THOUGHTS
I don't like to sleep because I see shadows in the dark.	I am in control of my thoughts. I know that I am safe at home in my bed.
My mom is taking me to the doctor today and I wasn't expecting it.	I will deal with whatever comes my way. I am strong and powerful!
I like fireworks but what if it's really loud?	I will remember a time when I was scared but I was able to power through it. I can bring ear protectors just in case.
My dad just dropped me off at a friend's house but what if he forgets to pick me up?	I will examine my worry as if I am a detective to see if there is any evidence that it's real. My dad never forgets to pick me up!
I like to wear fun clothes but what if kids tease me because of my style?	I like my style and will walk and talk with confidence.
I'm going to a new school this fall. What if I don't make any friends?	I can decide to be friendly and bring new friends into my life. I will focus on making friends instead of on my worry.

I Feel Worried! Tips for Kids on Overcoming Anxiety

WORRIED THOUGHTS	COPING THOUGHTS
What if I don't know what to do next and feel too shy to ask?	I can decide to solve my problems. I will stop the worry and take action and ask the question.
Uh oh! My teacher just told us that we have to give a book report in front of the whole class!	I can write my worry down and put it in my worry box and then talk to an adult about it later.
We're having a different schedule at school today. What should I do?	I can remember that worrying doesn't solve problems at all and only wastes a lot of energy. I can make myself a change-of-schedule card for today.
I'm going to a birthday party today and I may not know many of the kids.	I can focus on all the good things that happen and not the bad
My dad is late picking me up. I wonder if something happened to him.	I will focus on positive thoughts to keep the bad thoughts out of my brain.
My neighbors just got a dog and I'm afraid it will jump on me.	I can imagine that I have a TV in my brain and will change the channel from the worry channel to a fun and courageous channel when I am around the dog.

WORRIED THOUGHTS

COPING THOUGHTS

I hope my project is good enough. I tried to make it perfect but what if it isn't?

I can only try to do my best. No one is perfect.

I might need a shot when I go to the doctor next time and it will hurt.

I will take three deep belly breaths to relax my body, then count to three and the shot will be over just like that!

_____

_____

_____

I Feel Worried! Tips for Kids on Overcoming Anxiety

MAKE YOUR OWN EMOTIONS WHEEL

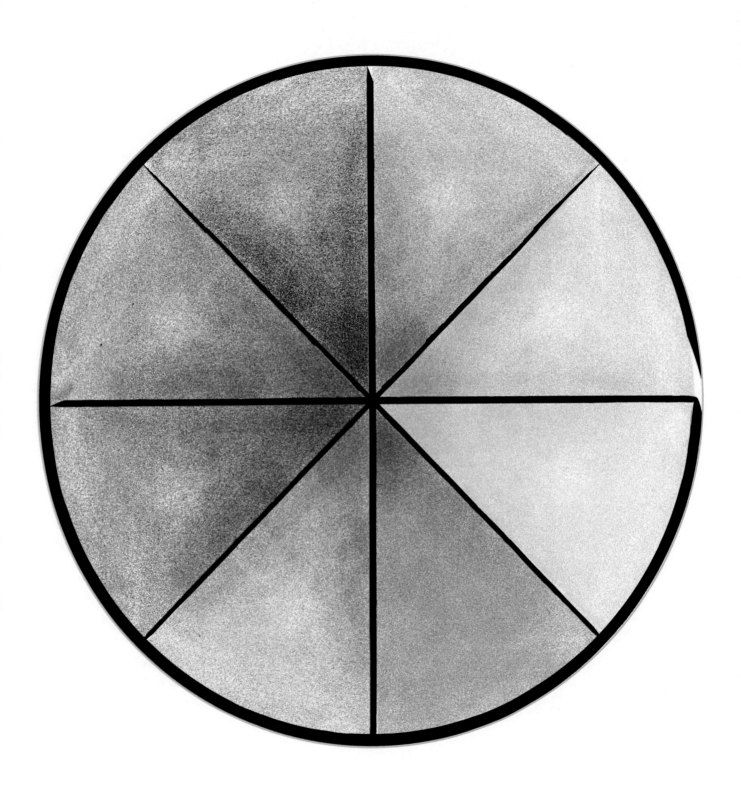

THAT'S IT!
THANK YOU SO MUCH FOR READING OUR BOOK!

We would love to hear what you thought about these tips and how they may have helped you manage your worried feelings.
We are also always interested in new ideas from kids that read our books!
Your mom, dad or guardian can help you write or email us.
howtomakeandkeepfriends@gmail.com
How to Make and Keep Friends
P.O. Box 312
Harvard, MA 01451

We would appreciate it if you would take a minute to review our book on Amazon. We learn a great deal from our readers and your comments!

ABOUT THE AUTHORS

Donna Shea and Nadine Briggs are both accomplished social educators. They each facilitate friendship groups at their respective centers in Massachusetts. Both Nadine and Donna are parents of children with special needs.

Donna and Nadine consult with schools, parent groups, and human service agencies. They are also seasoned public speakers and travel to bring workshops and seminars to schools, conferences, and other venues across the country.

Donna and Nadine are certified in bullying prevention through the Massachusetts Aggression Reduction Center and are creators of the How to Make & Keep Friends Bullying Prevention Initiative to provide classroom training and team building for school systems.

We would love to receive your feedback on our books, to speak with you about providing programming in your area, and to keep in touch about new books and materials.

Find us on Facebook, Twitter and Instagram!

The newly updated and revised edition of How to Make & Keep Friends: Tips for Kids to Overcome 50 Common Social Challenges By Nadine Briggs and Donna Shea offers social skills and friendship advice presented in an easy to read, reference guide format. Included are simple and immediately actionable tips to navigate common social situations that can be challenging, including:

- How to Join a Group
- Handling Rejection and Exclusion
- Being a Good Guest and Host

- How to Safely Handle Angry Feelings
- Working Things Out & Sharing Fairly
- Playground Success... And much more!

In this updated edition we have taken the feedback from our reviews and readers and added why learning each of these skills is important along with practice questions to inspire discussion and role playing of different social situations with children.

How to Make and Keep Friends: Helping Your Child Achieve Social Success is a how-to manual for parents of children with social challenges. The easy-to-read format clearly outlines common barriers that hinder friendships, provides actionable tips for overcoming those barriers, and includes suggested language for parents to use to provide support to their kids during unstructured social interactions. Parents play a key role in the formation of friendships. How to Make and Keep Friends: Helping Your Child Achieve Social Success shows parents how to guide their children toward true and meaningful friendship connections.

The I Feel Mad! anger workbook provides simple, actionable, and proven strategies to help kids manage angry feelings. In this workbook, your child will learn:
- the anger rule to follow and what he or she can and cannot do when feeling angry
- that anger is a normal emotion we all have, but managing anger appropriately is a critical life skill
- how to identify the physical sensations of anger and implement strategies before it becomes too hot to handle
- a menu of safe strategies to choose from when angry situations arise
- effective problem-solving skills and specific reactions to replace an angry response.

Made in the USA
San Bernardino, CA
05 November 2016